Church Architecture

A Catholic Adult Coloring Book

Go to **casoncatholic.com** to find more coloring books.

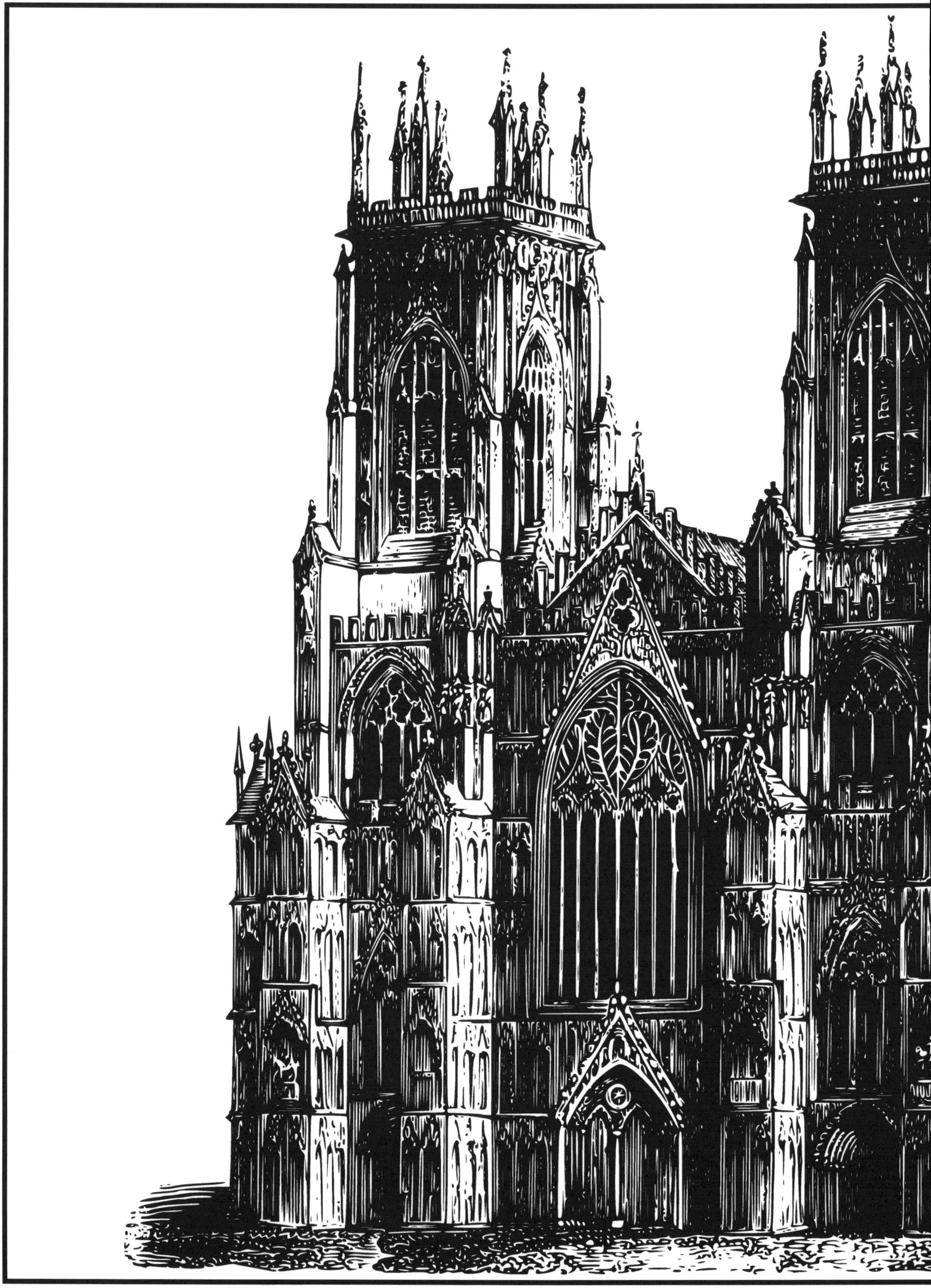

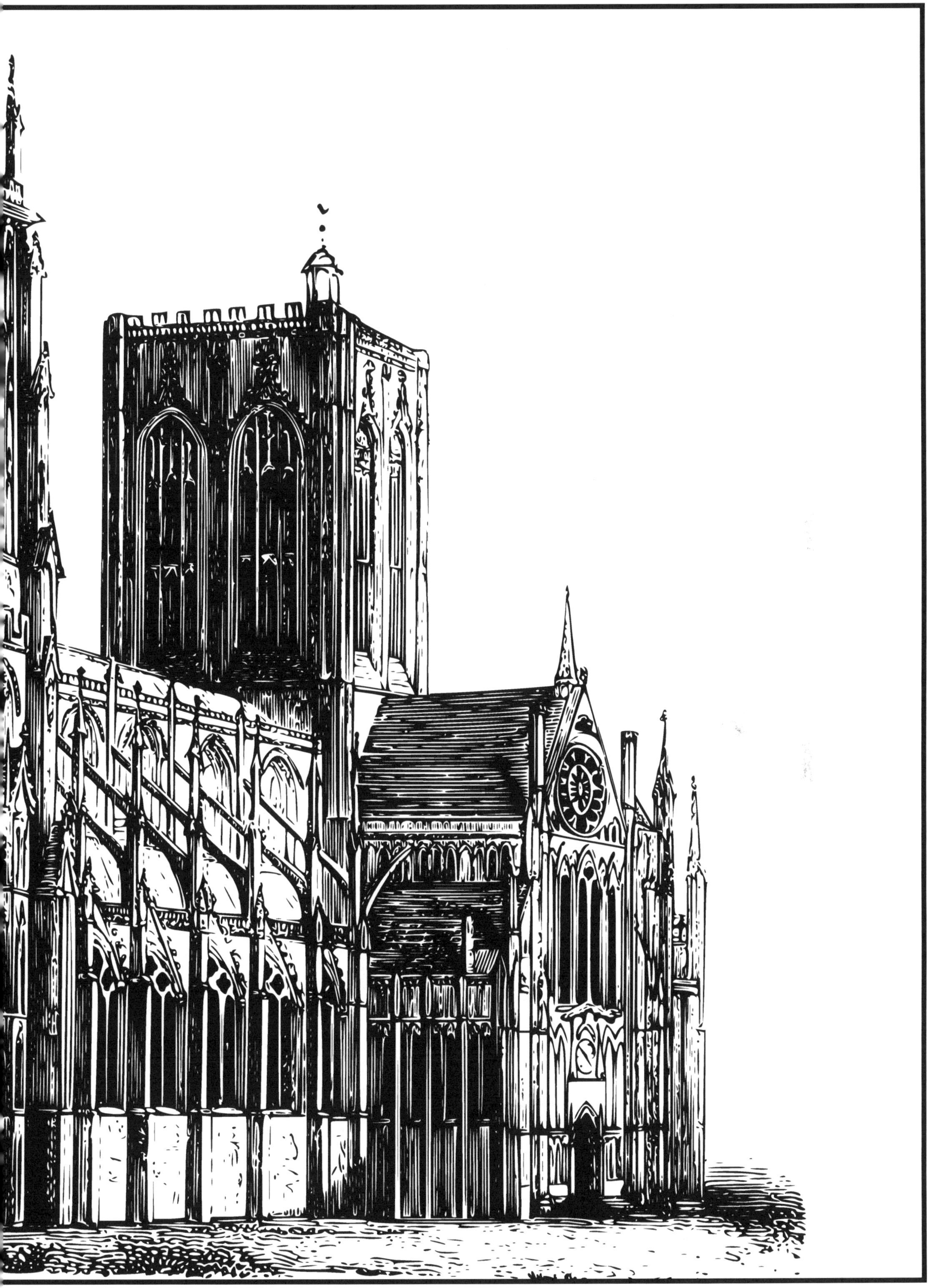

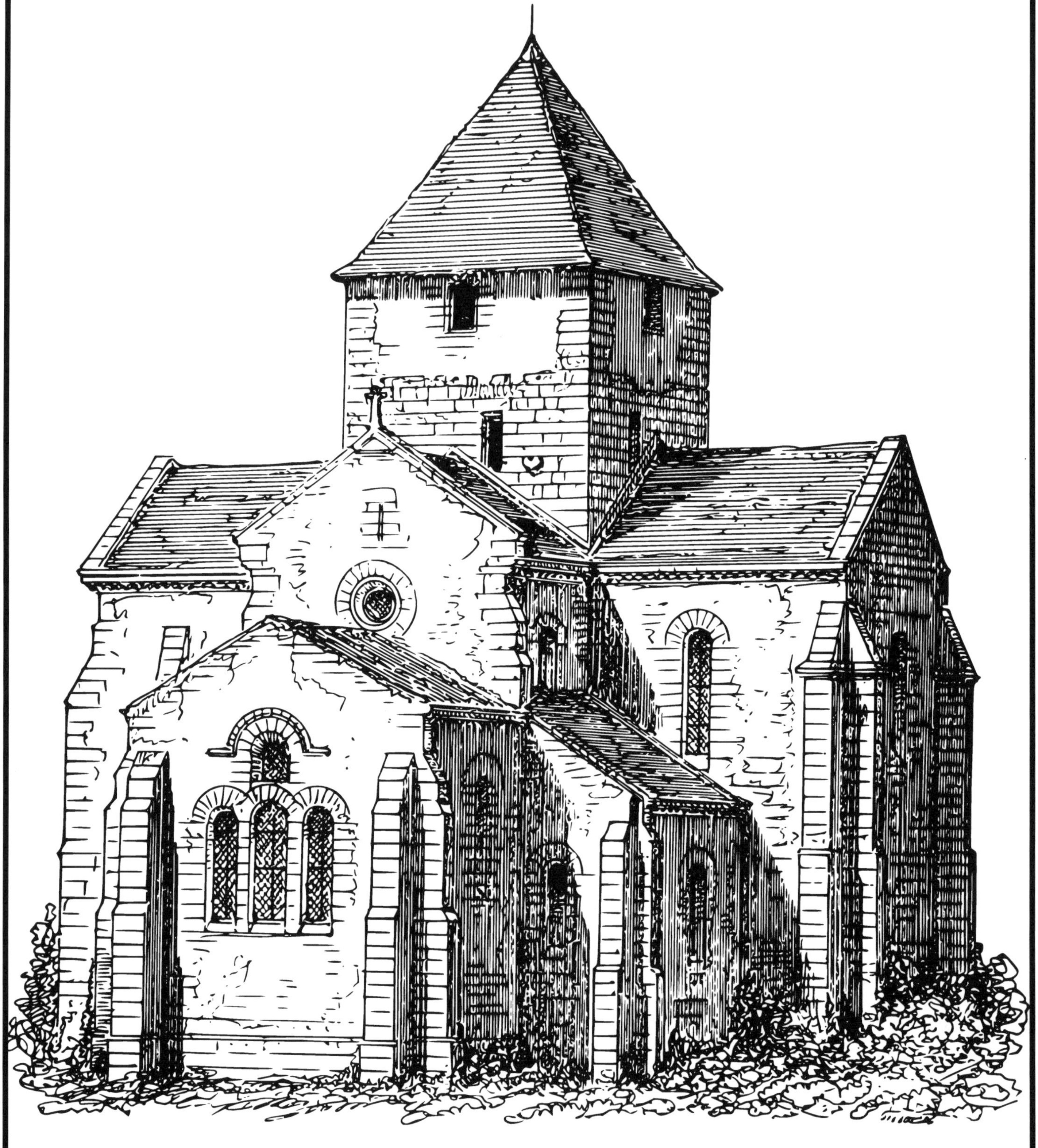

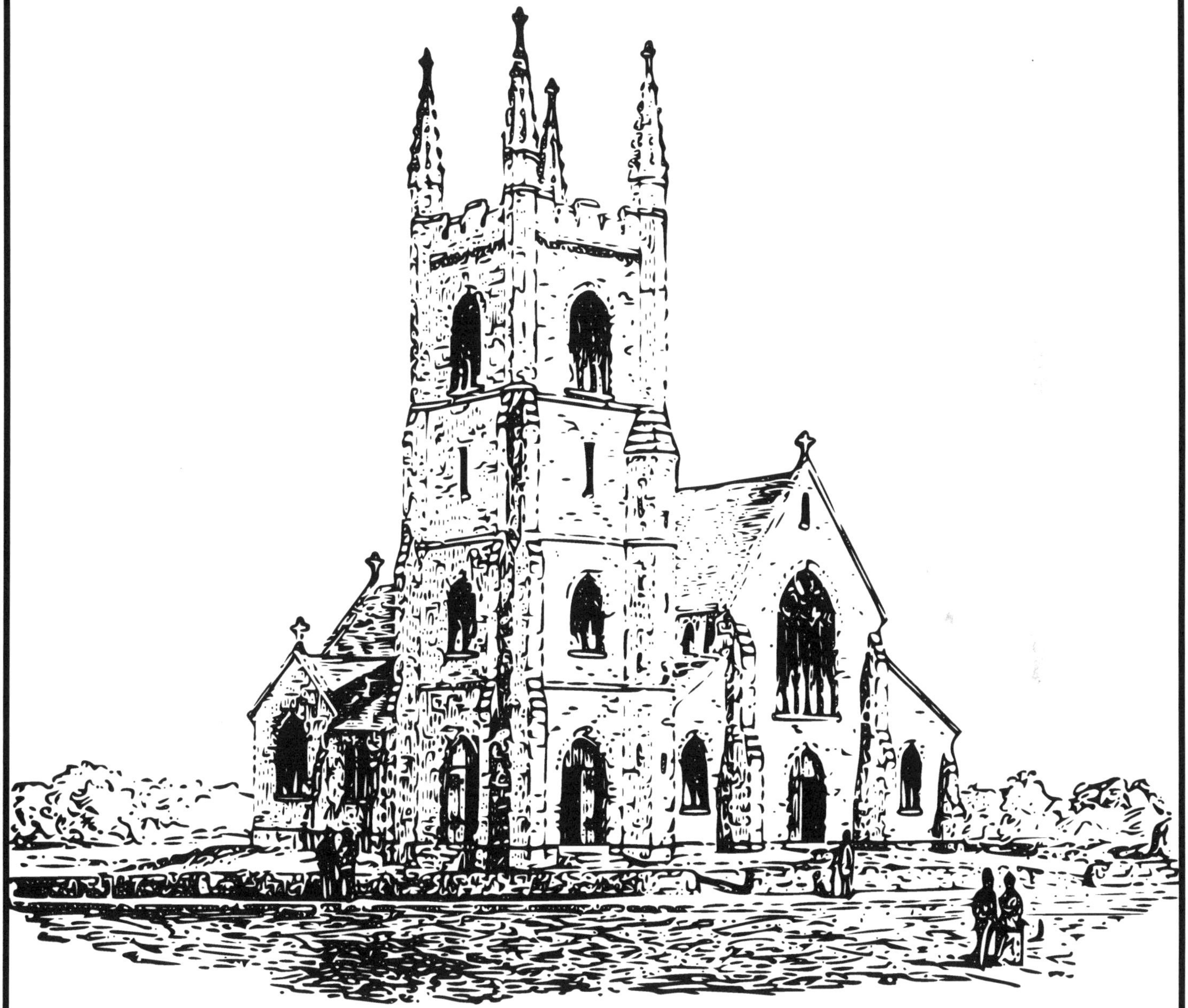

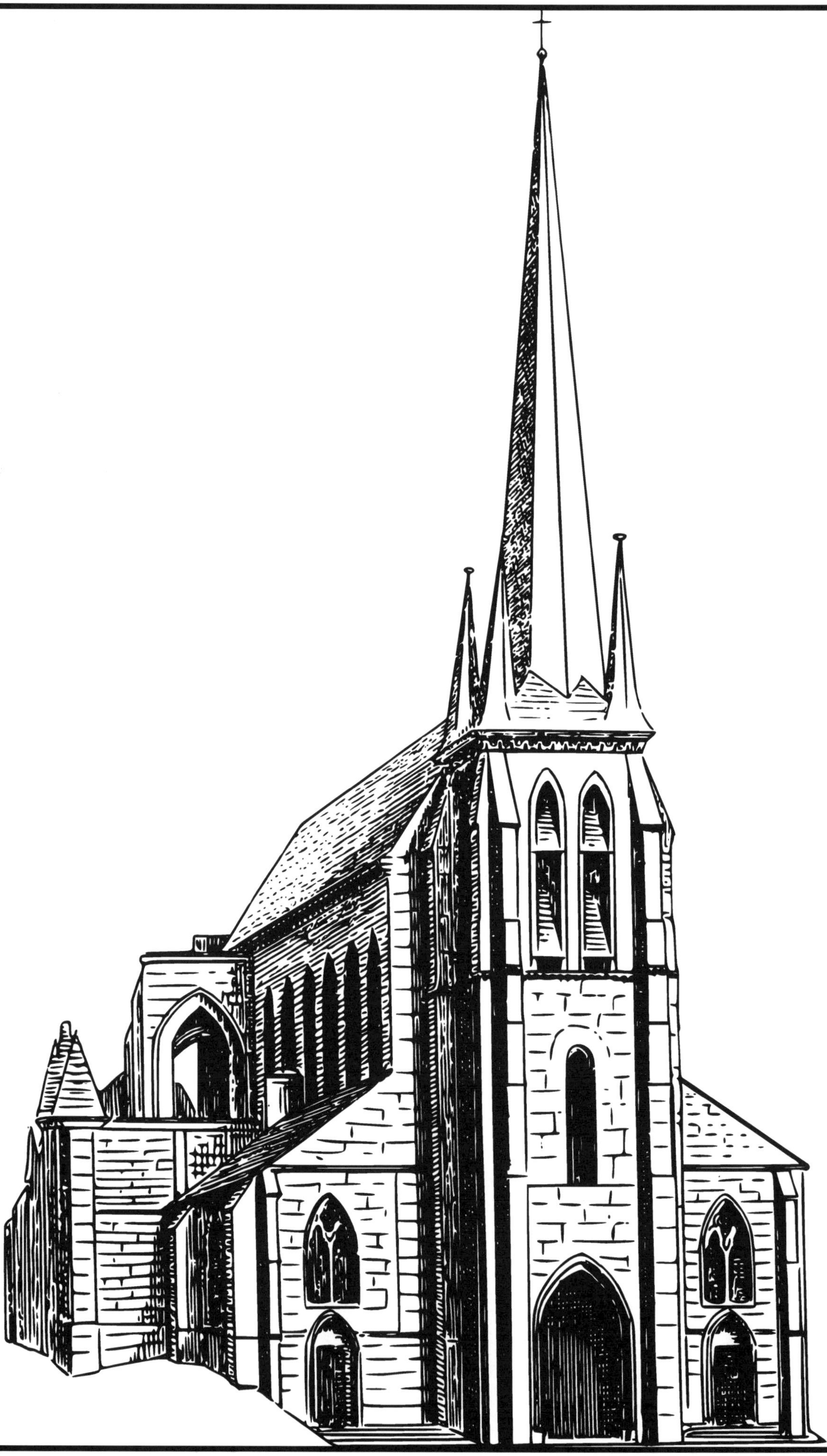

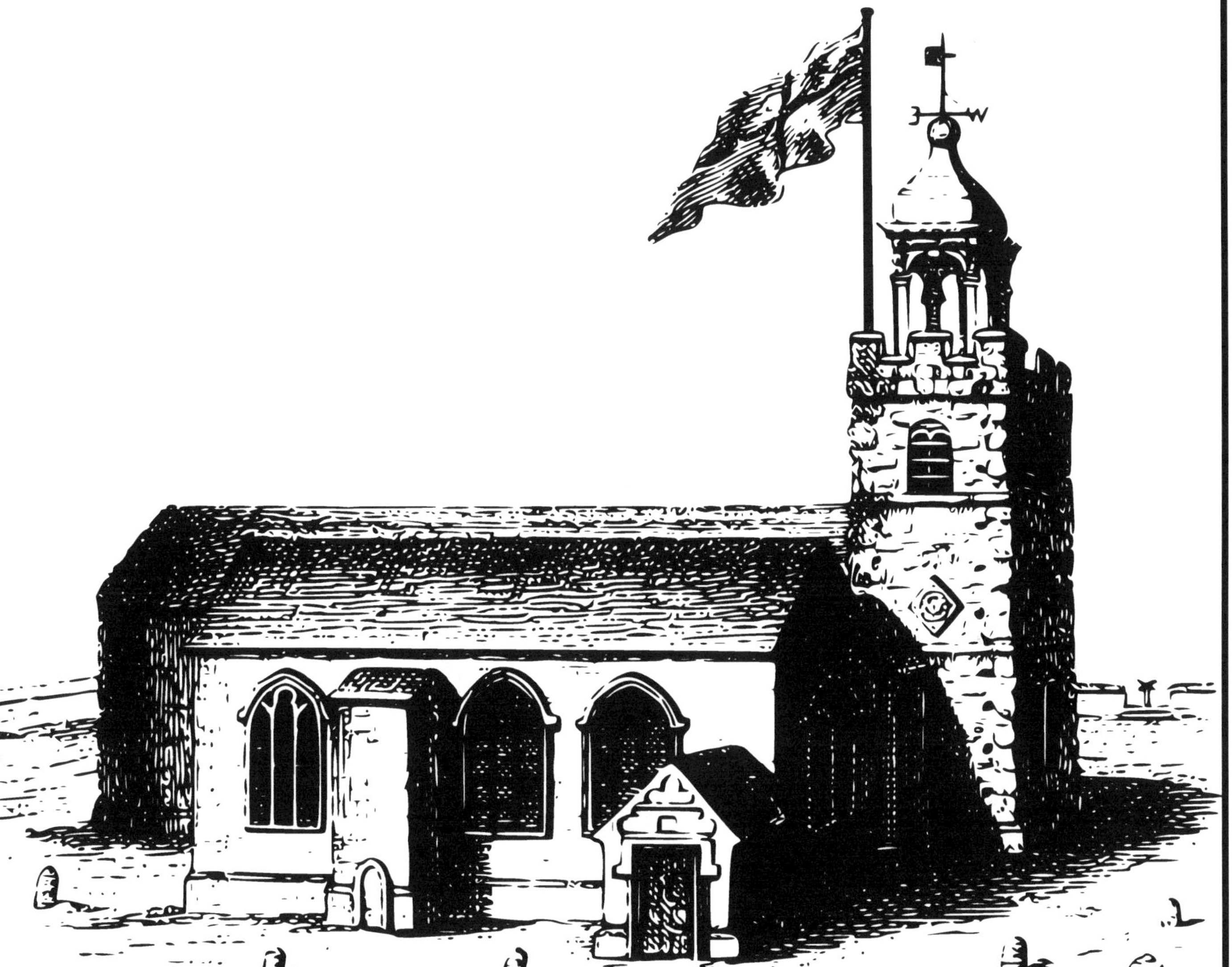

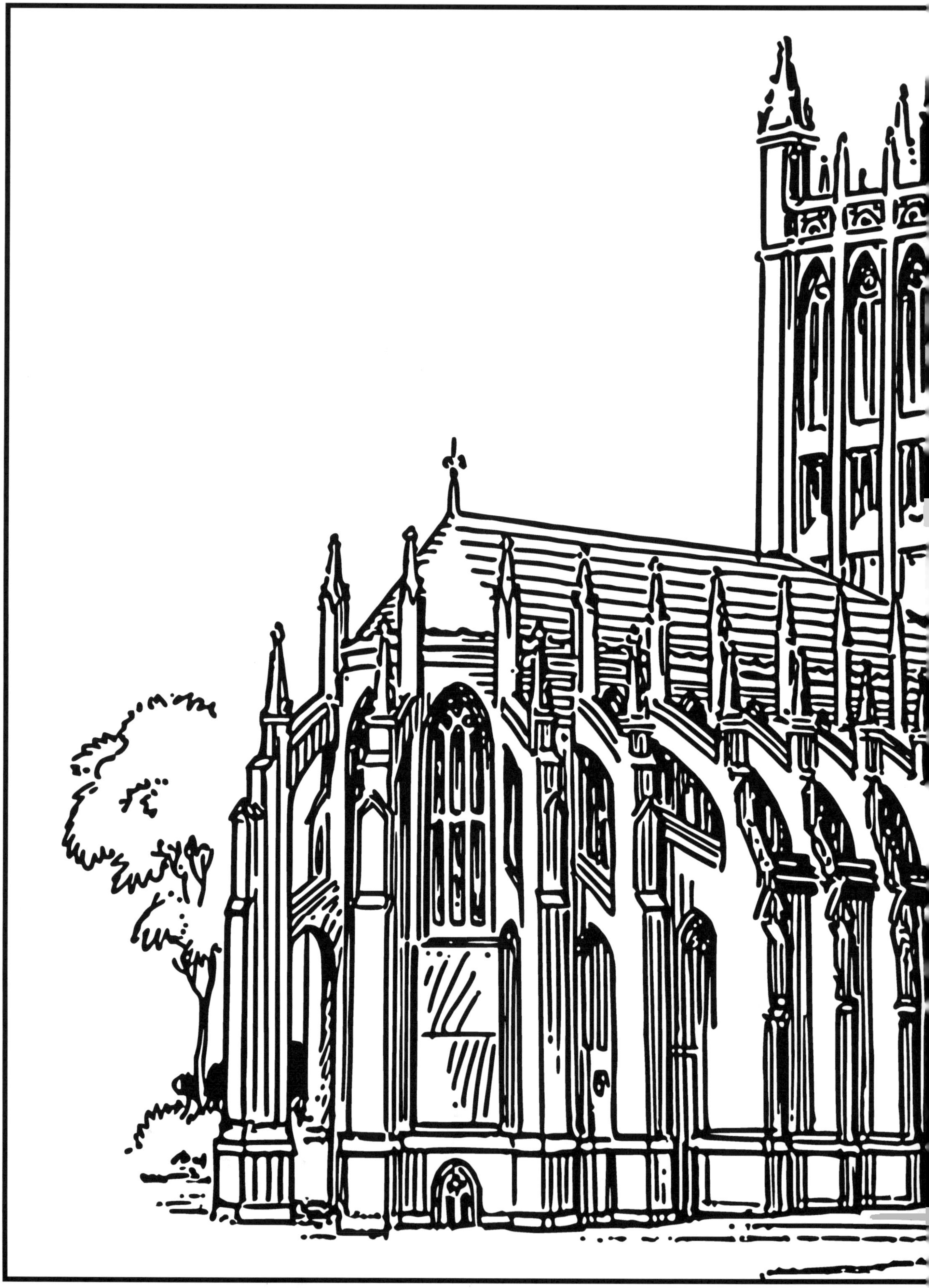

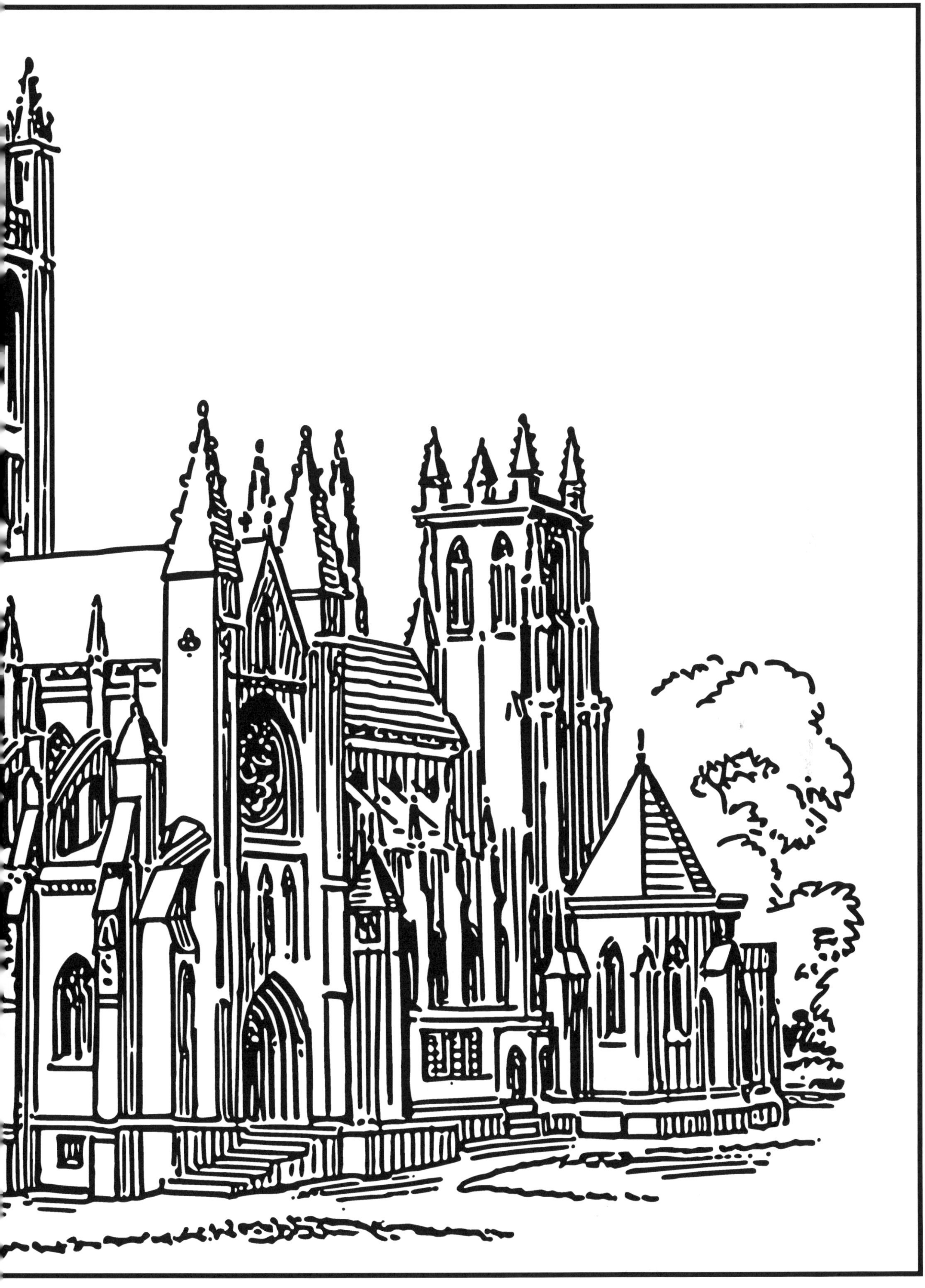

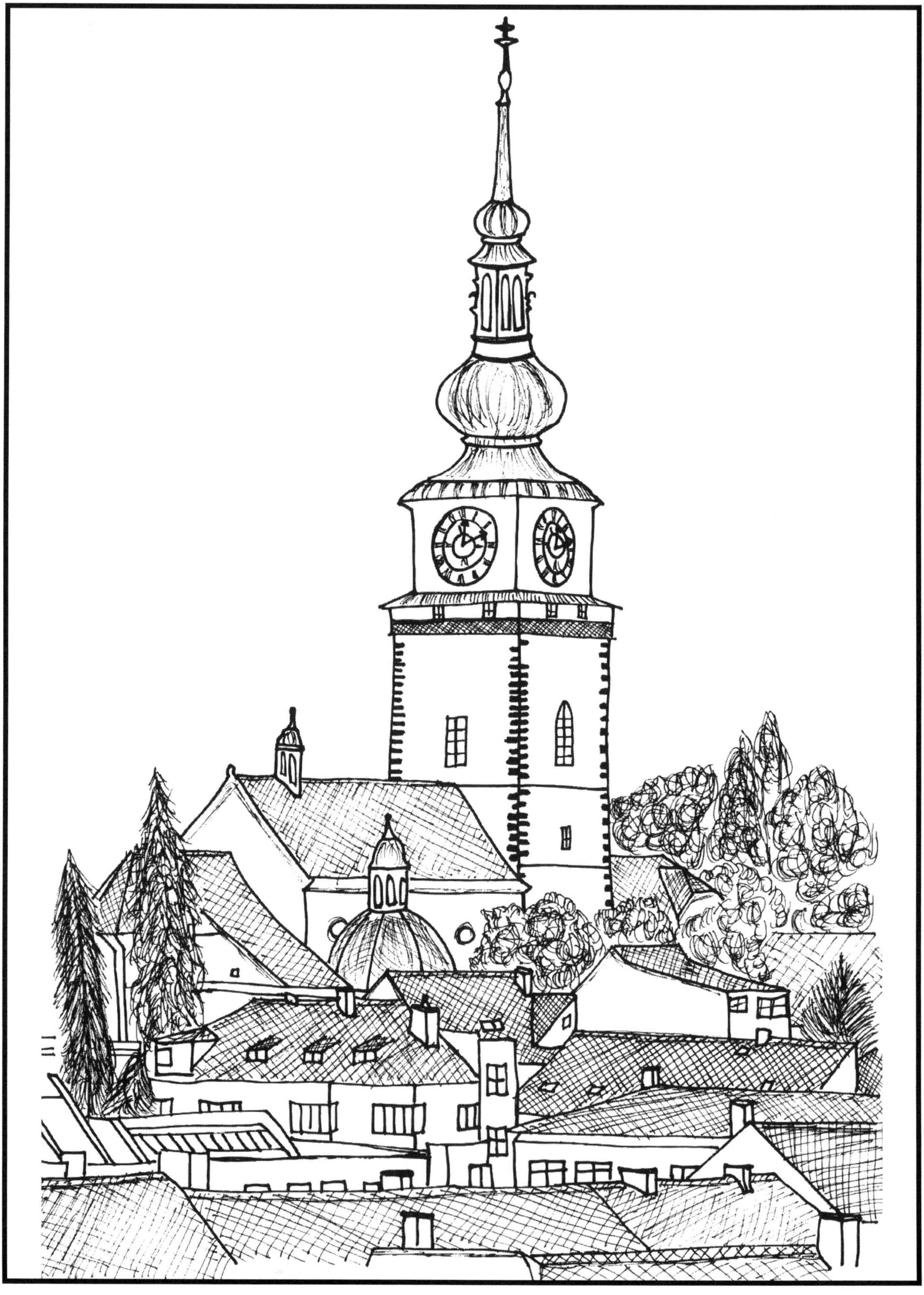

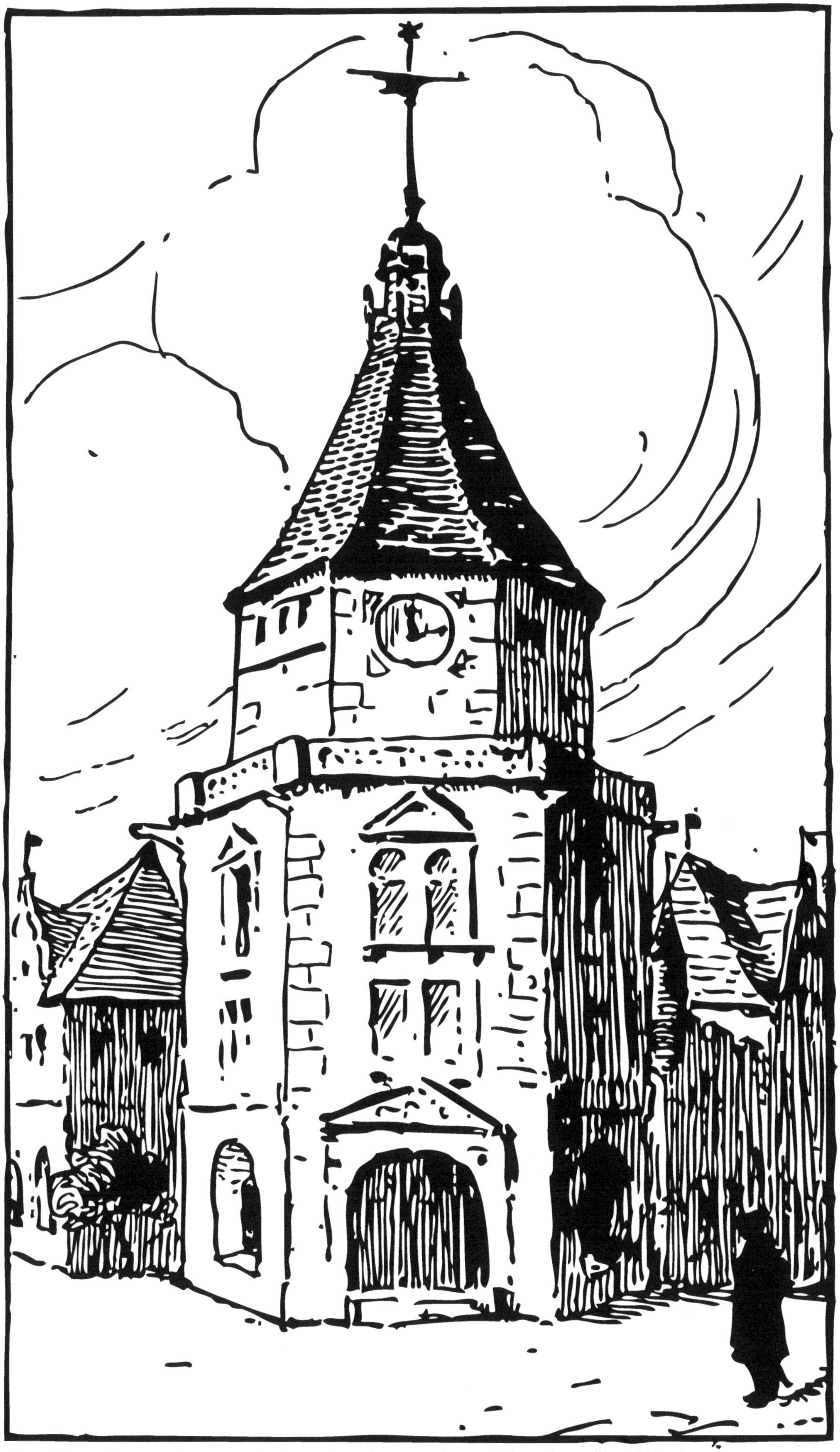

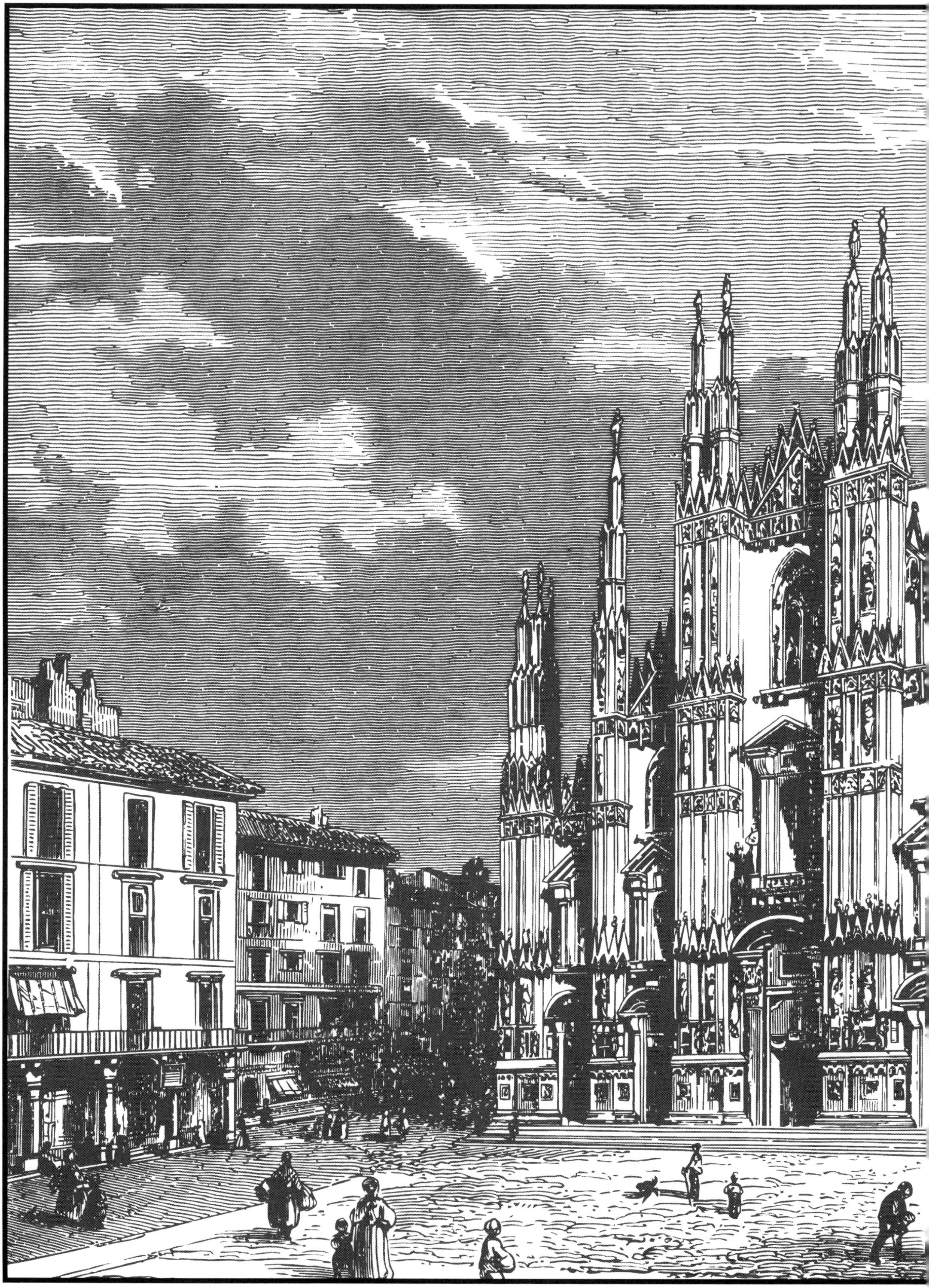

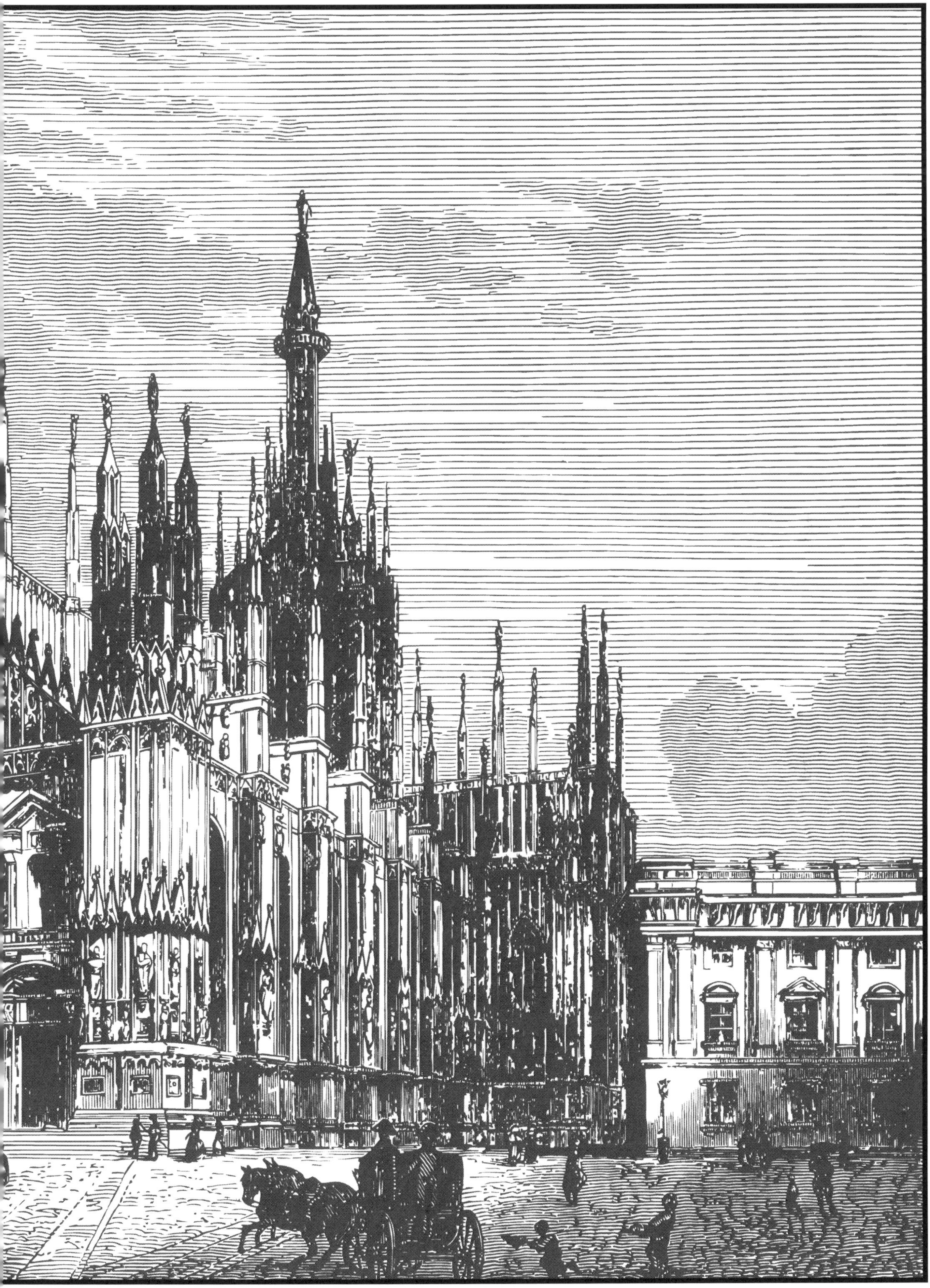

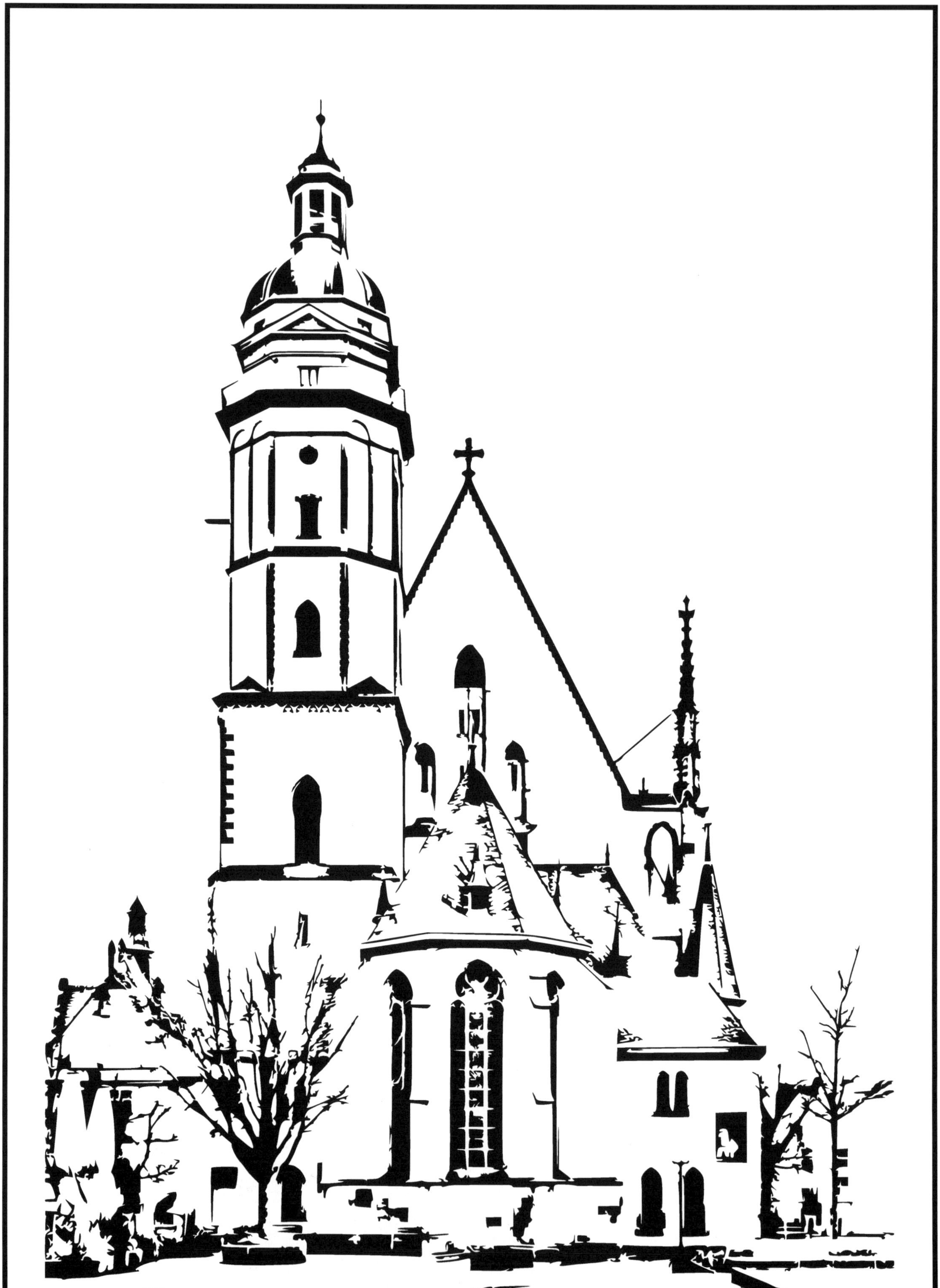

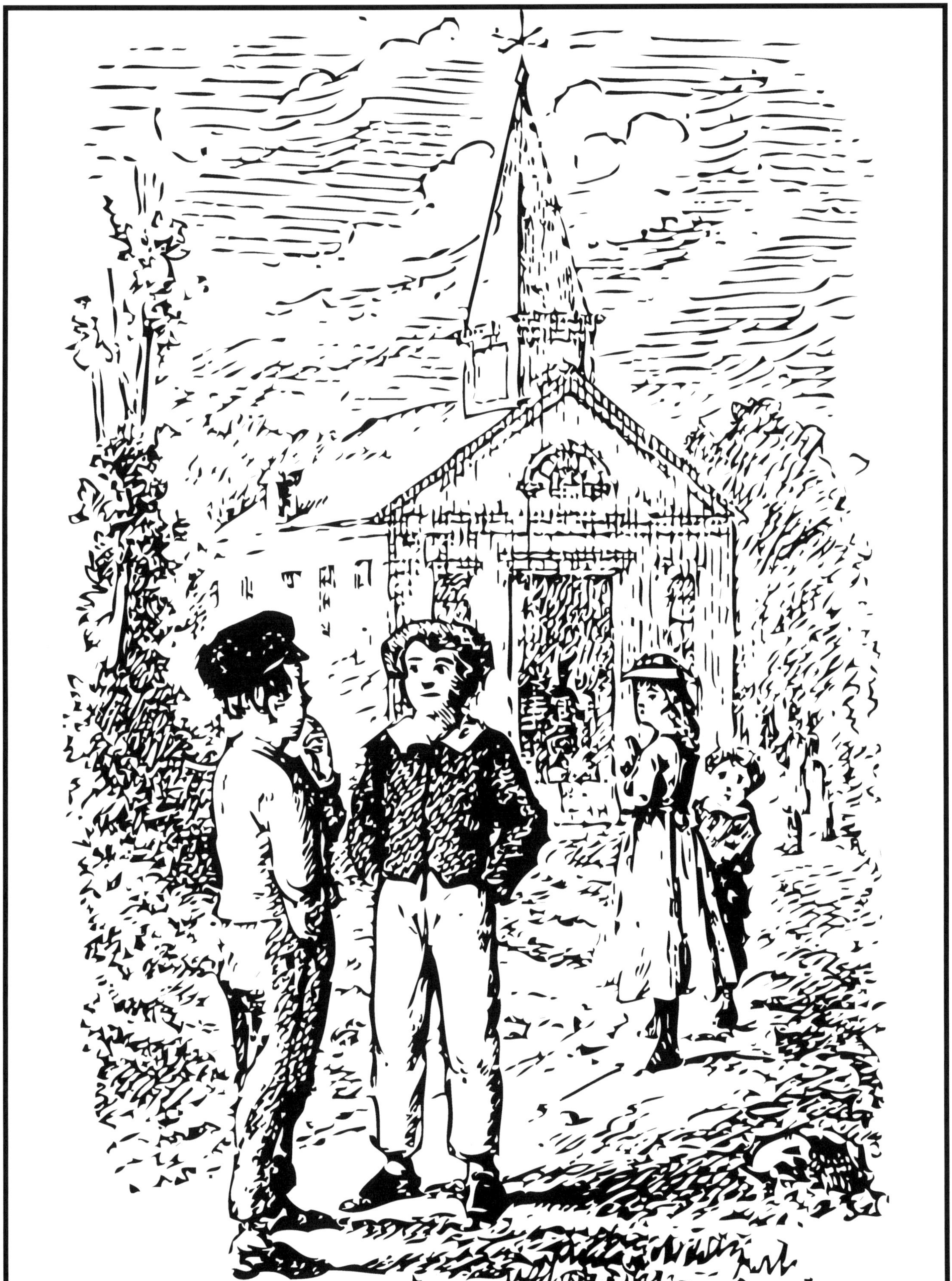

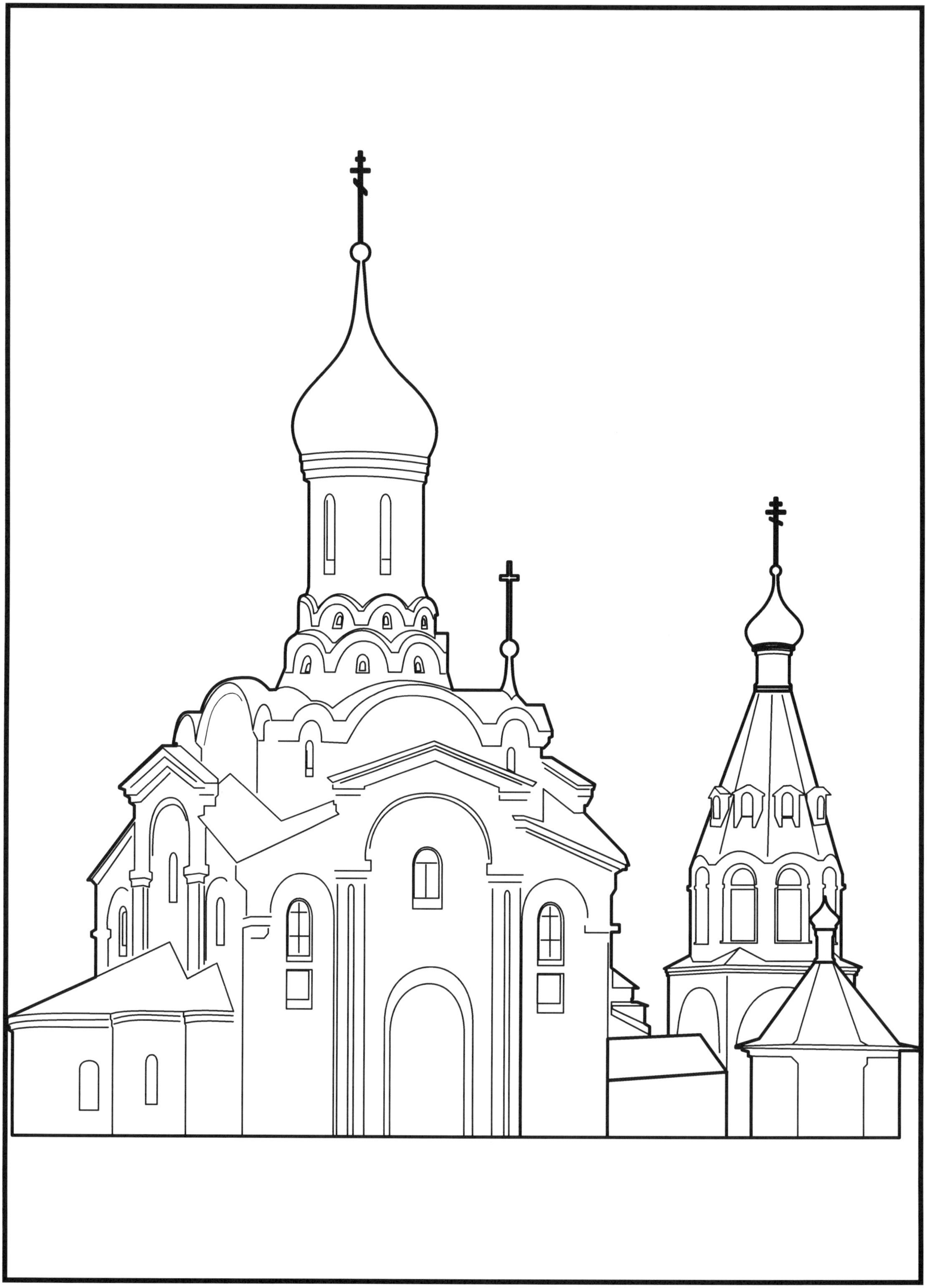

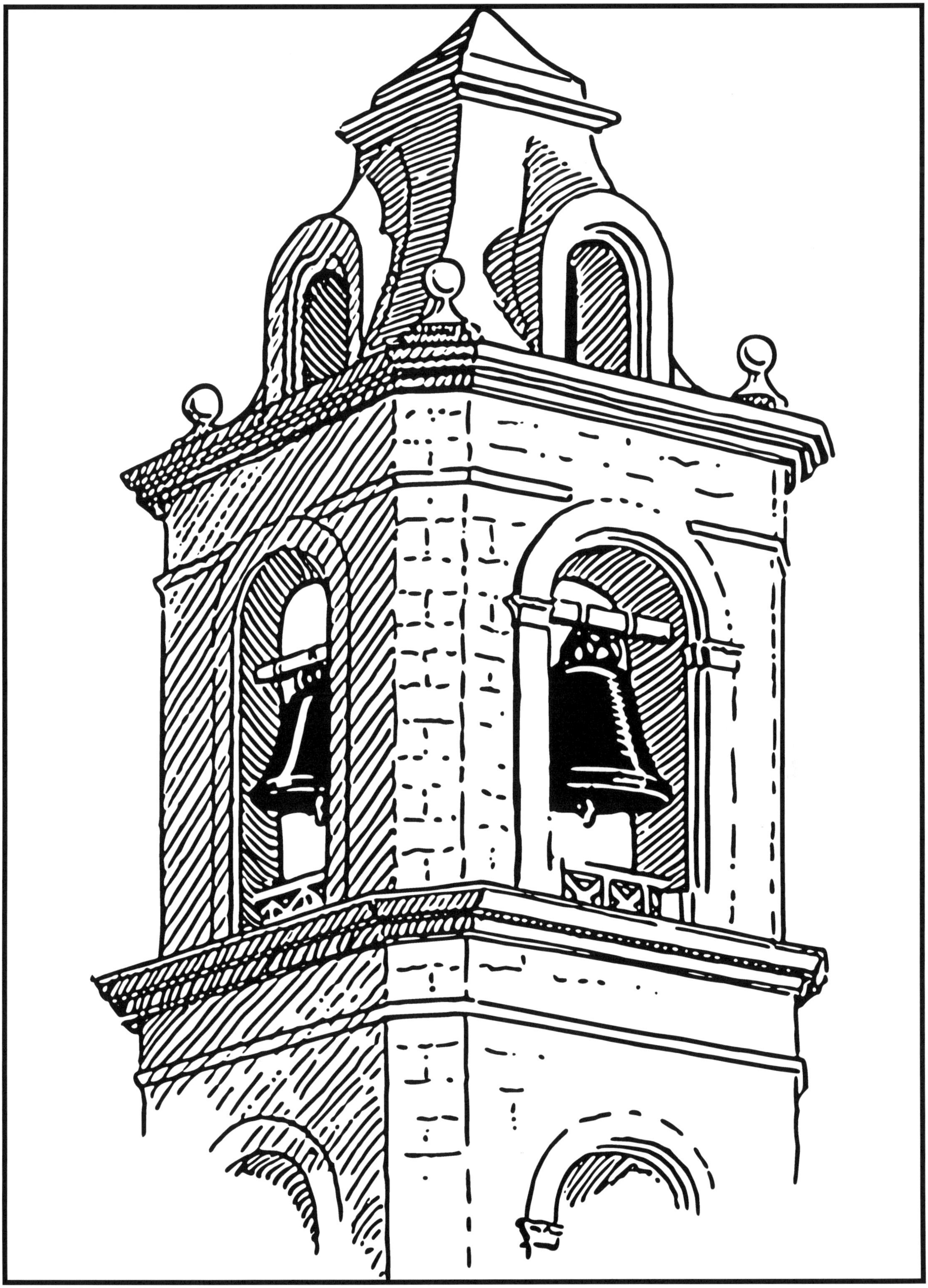

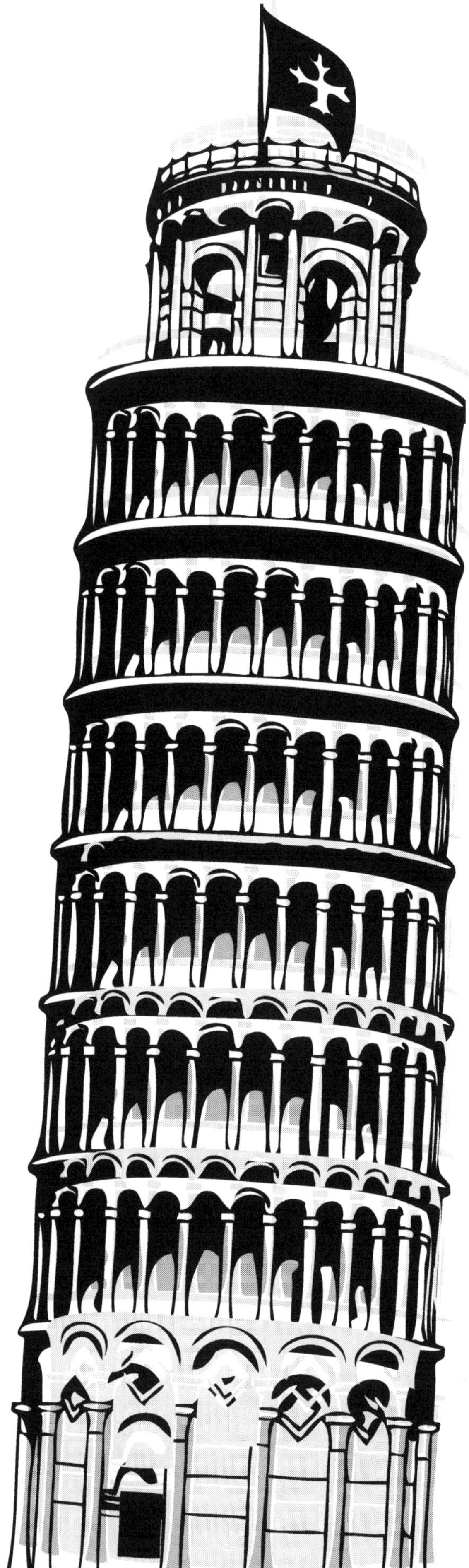

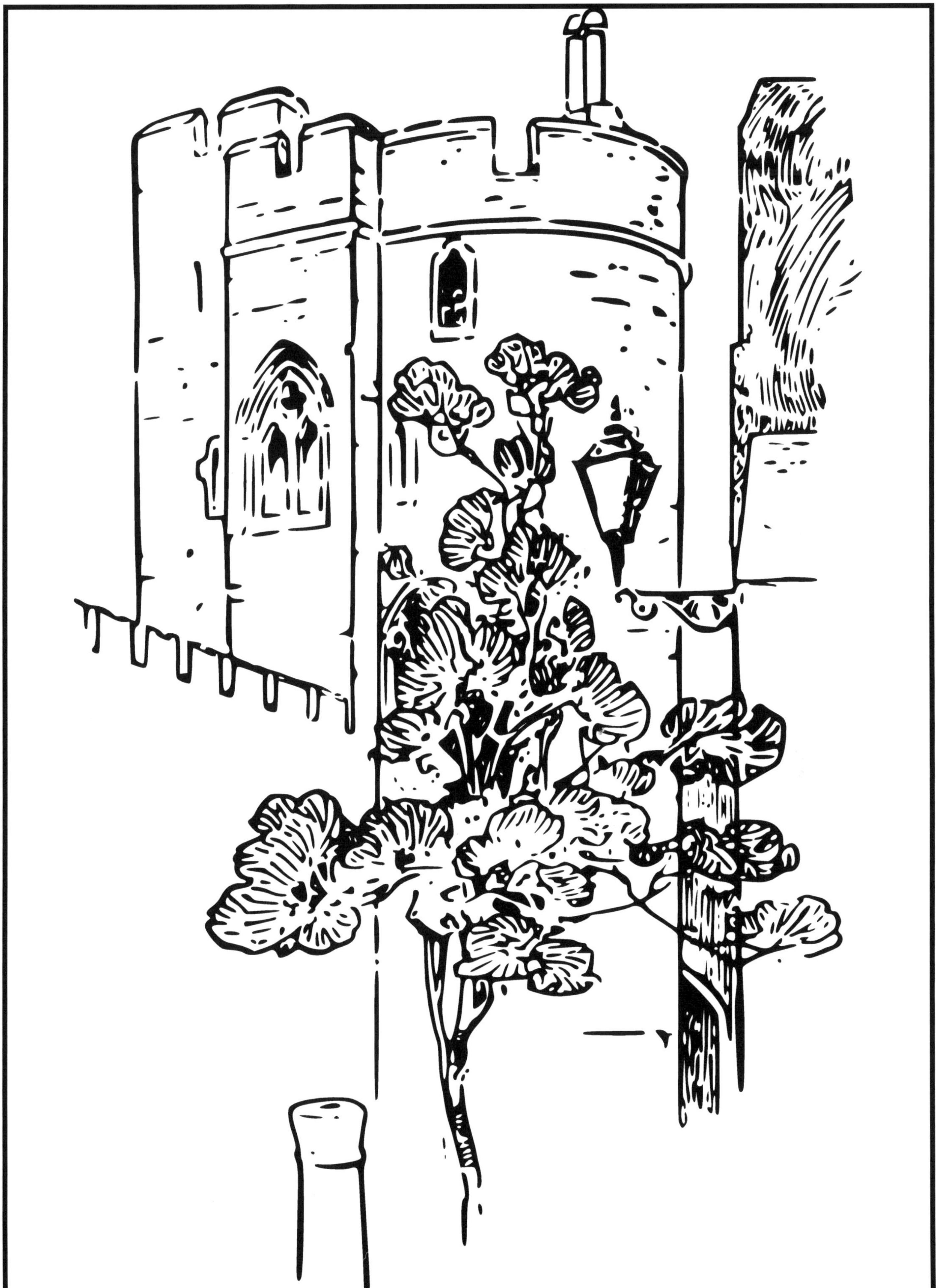

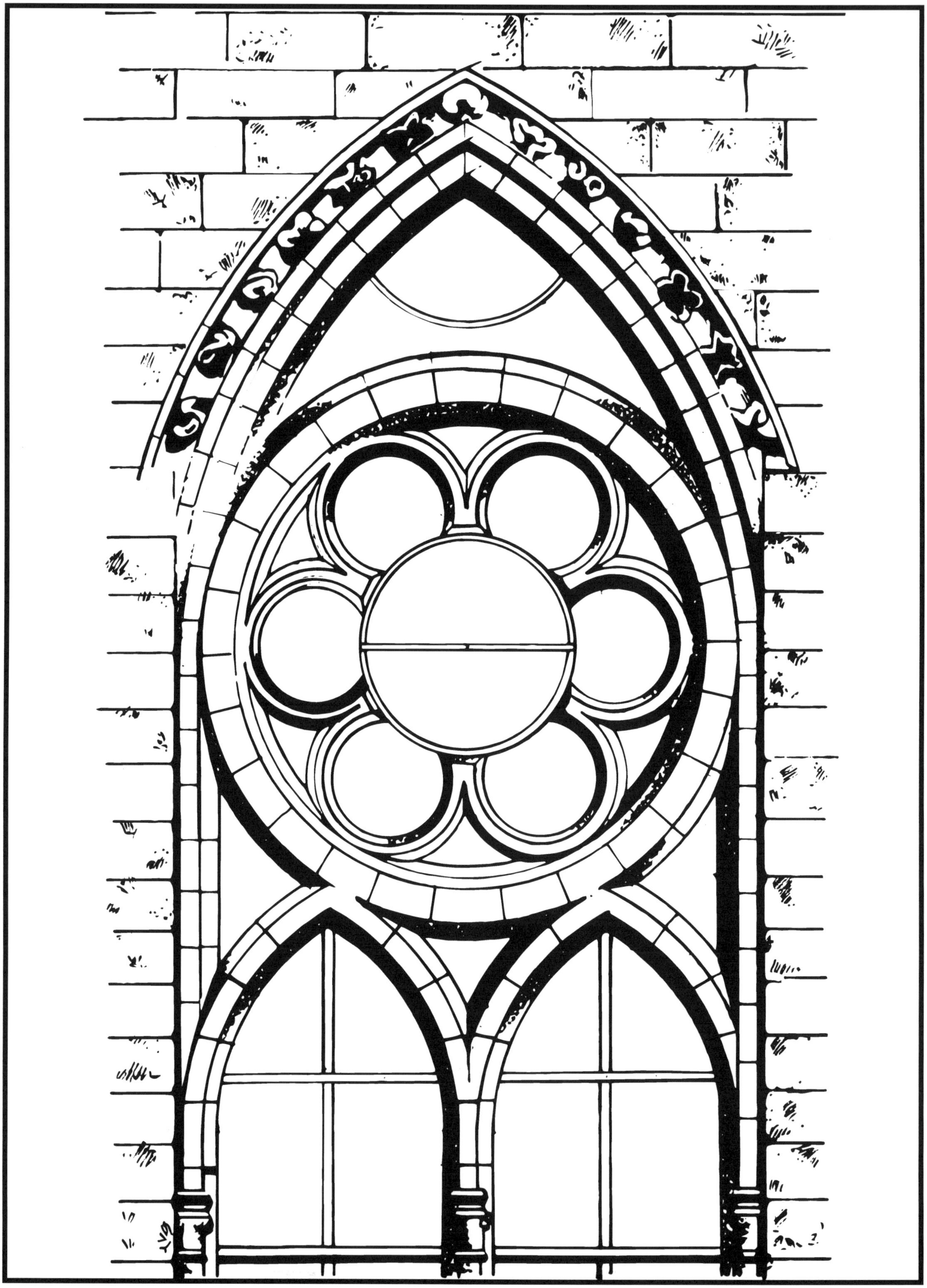

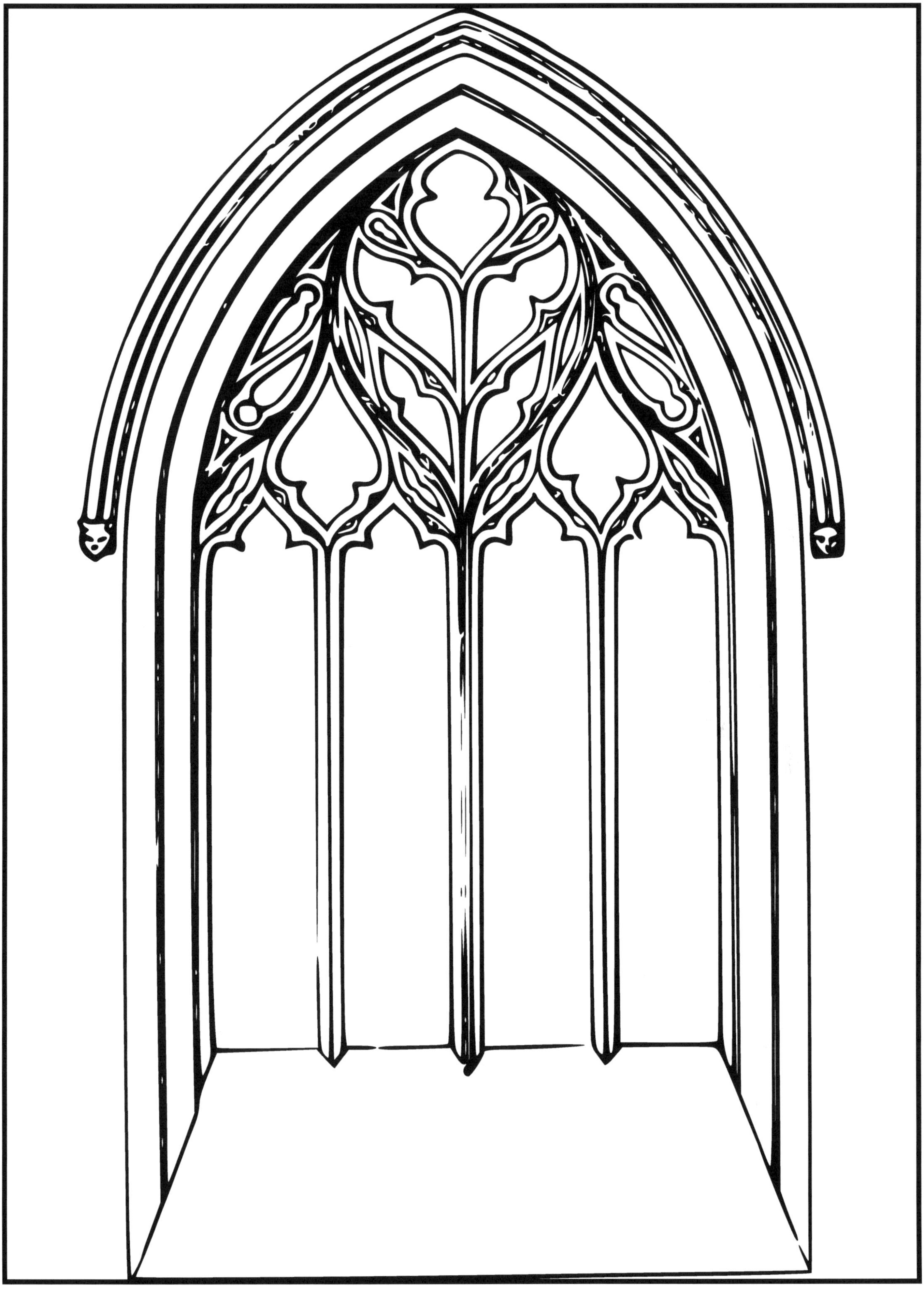

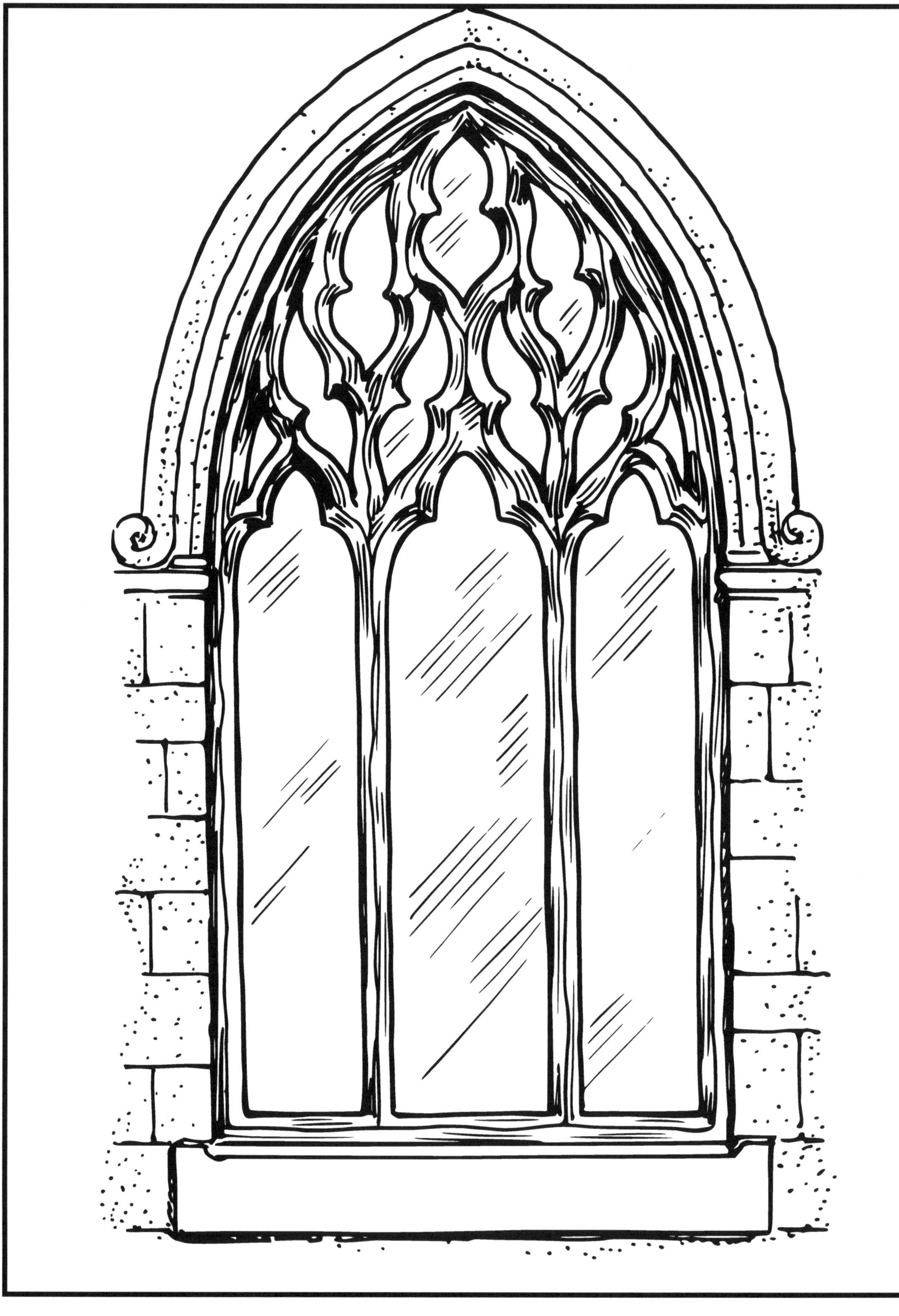

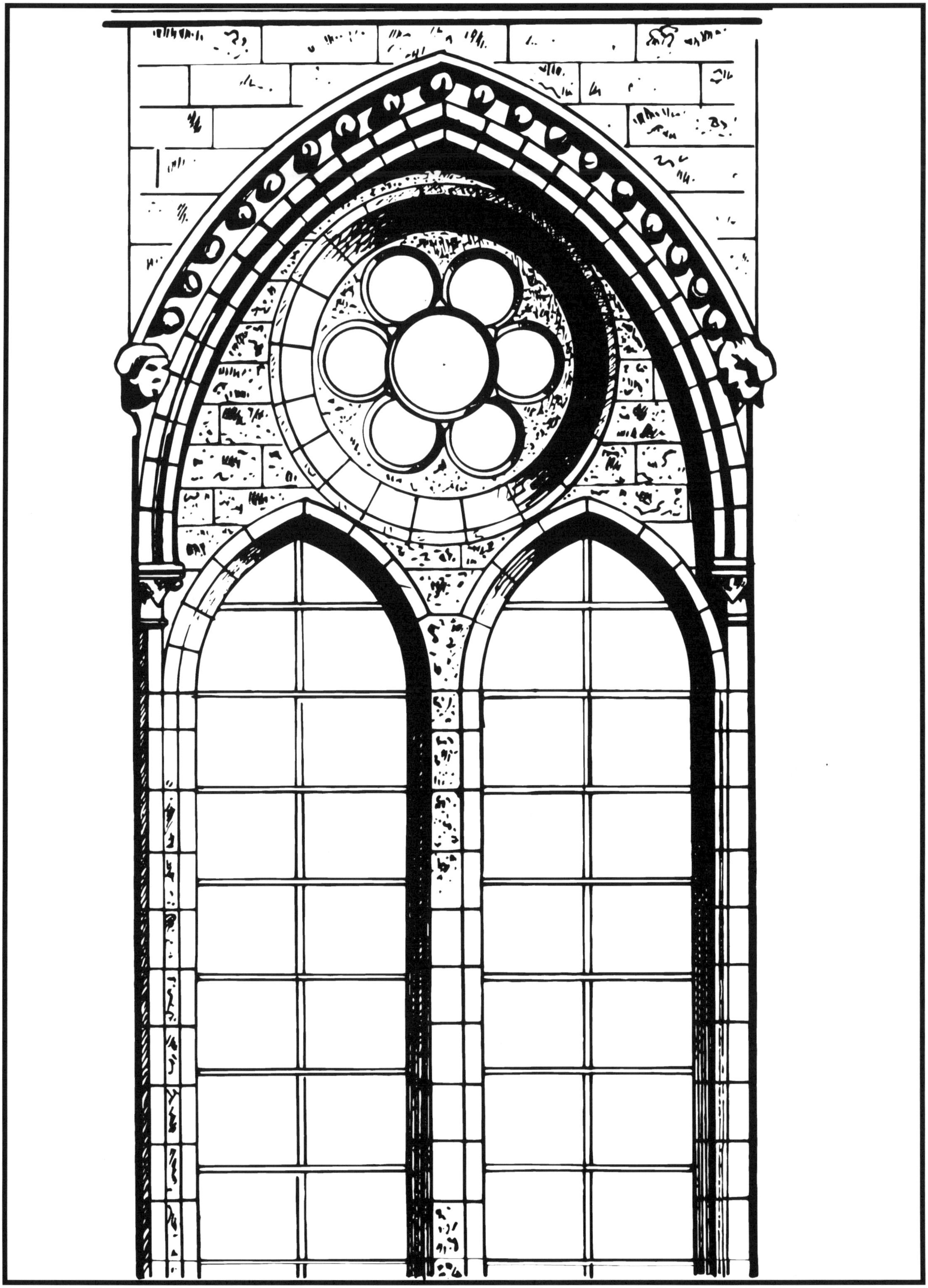

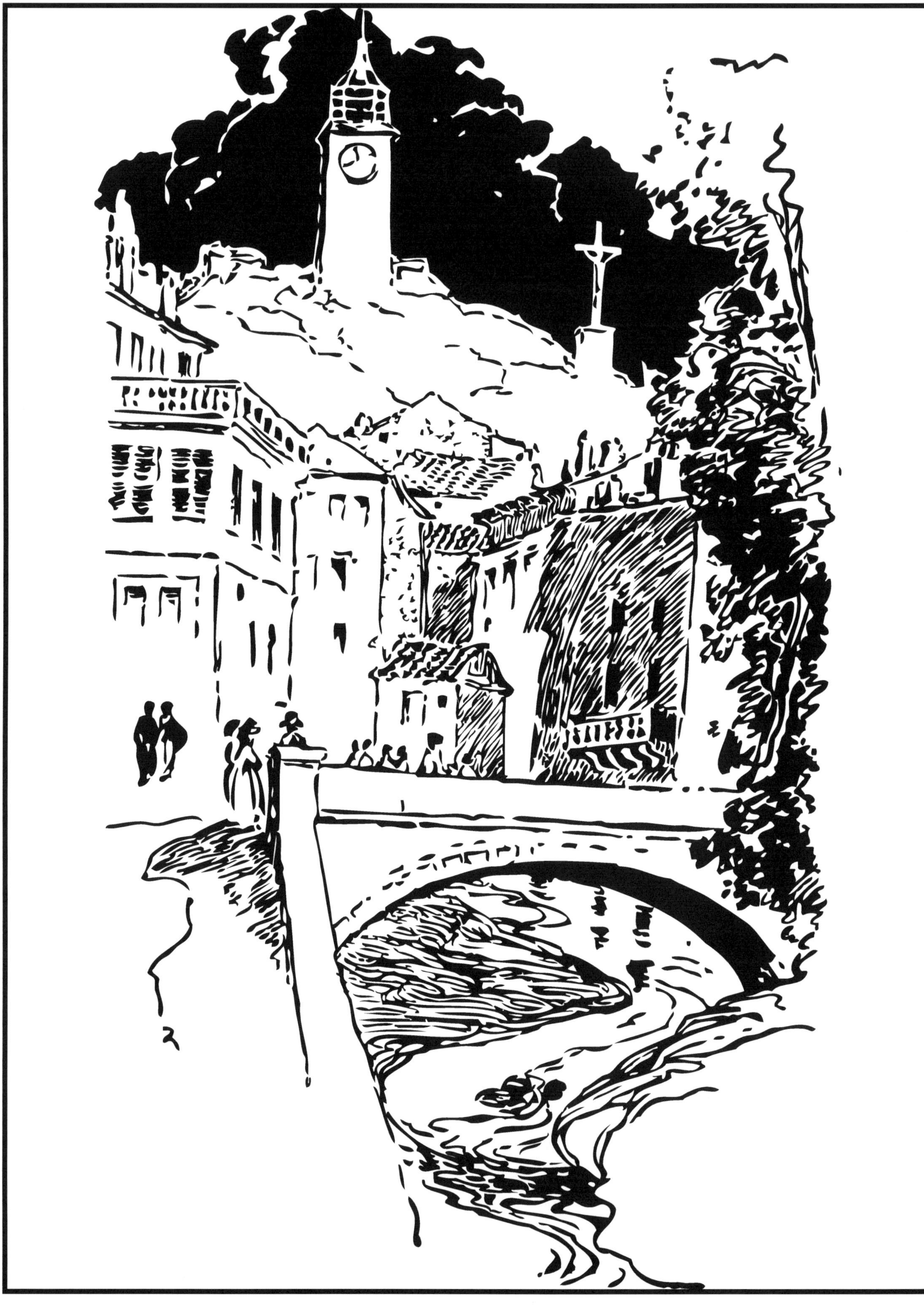

Made in United States
Orlando, FL
19 September 2024

51673668R00015